Shakespeare
On Love

Shakespeare
On Love

Quotations from the Plays and Poems

*Compiled and with
an Introduction
by George Weinberg*

St. Martin's Press
New York

www. stmartins.com

Production Editor: David Stanford Burr

Design by Dawn Niles

Library of Congress Cataloging-in-Publication Data

Shakespeare, William, 1564–1616.
        Shakespeare on love : quotations from the plays and
poems / selected and with an introduction by George Weinberg.
            p.   cm.
        1. Shakespeare, William, 1564–1616—
Quotations.   2. Love—Quotations, maxims, etc.
I. Weinberg, George H.   II. Title.
    PR2771.W44   1991
    822.3′3—dc20   90-49188
                                                    CIP

        ISBN 13: 978-0-312-05514-1
        ISBN 10: 0-312-05514-5

10   9   8

Table of Contents

Introduction   vii

What Is Love?   1
The Mystery of Love   4
Love's Magic   5
Courtship   7
First Love   11
Love's Eagerness   12
The Pursuit of Love   13
Lover's Wiles   16
Love's Progress   18
Obsessive Love   19
Love's Folly   20
Love's Rocky Course   23
The Kiss   24
All Encompassing Love   25
Contrary Love   27
The Fullness of Love   30
In Praise of the Beloved   33

Love's Delusions   35

Love's Abandon   36

Mockery of Love   38

Passionate Love   40

Unrequited Love   43

Love's Torment   45

Love's Secrecy   50

Loquacious Love   52

Parting   53

Vows of Love   55

Love Disdained   58

Forbidden Love   60

Love's Frailty   61

Jealousy   63

The Power of Love   66

The Curse of Love   67

Love's Understanding   69

Love Lost   70

Betrayal   72

Chastity   75

Lust   77

Self Love   79

Unending Love   81

About Shakespeare   85

Introduction

Most people would agree that William Shakespeare is without rival as a playwright and poet. However, he was also the world's greatest psychologist, with an uncanny ability to see and describe people's most subtle emotional states.

Shakespeare's poetic insights seem never to lose their freshness. Generations have turned to him for the language to express their own experiences. His influence is everywhere.

In the last century, when England ruled a mighty empire, the essayist, Thomas Carlyle, observed that England could lose that empire and still remain England: "But this Shakespeare does not go, he lasts forever with us; we cannot give up our Shakespeare."

Shakespeare wrote extensively about love: its exuberance, its glory, its sadness, its ironies, its vicissitudes. He found apt language to convey many facets of love. He described its whirling ecstasy, its fullness, its obsessive aspect. He gave us words to make its uncertainty endurable, to lighten the pain of rejection and even betrayal.

In this book are collected some of Shakespeare's greatest writings on love, a subject that requires supreme gifts of anyone who wishes to write about it. Surely, no other writer has ever made such a foray into this magical world and returned with so much of value. No one else could.

—GEORGE WEINBERG

Come, madam wife, sit by my side, and let the world slip, we shall ne'er be younger.

The Taming of the Shrew (Induction.2)

What Is
Love?

Love is a smoke made with the fume of sighs,
Being purg'd, a fire sparkling in lovers' eyes,
Being vex'd, a sea nourish'd with loving tears.
What is it else? a madness most discreet,
A choking gall, and a preserving sweet.

The Tragedy of Romeo and Juliet (1.1)

Love sought is good, but given unsought is better.

Twelfth Night, or What You Will (3.1)

What is love? 'Tis not hereafter;
Present mirth hath present laughter;
        What's to come is still unsure.
In delay there lies no plenty,
Then come kiss me sweet and twenty;
        Youth's a stuff will not endure.

Twelfth Night, or What You Will (2.3)

1

Love is like a child,
That longs for every thing that he can come by.

The Two Gentlemen of Verona (3.1)

Love is a familiar; Love is a devil; there is
no evil angel but Love.

Love's Labor's Lost (1.2)

Love's feeling is more soft and sensible
Than are the tender horns of cockled snails.
Love's tongue proves dainty Bacchus gross in taste.
For valor, is not Love a Hercules,
Still climbing trees in the Hesperides?
Subtile as Sphinx, as sweet and musical
As bright Apollo's lute, strung with his hair.
And when Love speaks, the voice of all the gods
Make heaven drowsy with the harmony.

Love's Labor's Lost (4.3)

love, first learned in a lady's eyes,
Lives not alone immured in the brain,
But with the motion of all elements,
Courses as swift as thought in every power,
And gives to every power a double power,
Above their functions and their offices.
It adds a precious seeing to the eye:

2

A lover's eyes will gaze an eagle blind.
A lover's ear will hear the lowest sound,
. . . .
Never durst poet touch a pen to write
Until his ink were temp'red with Love's sighs:
O then his lines would ravish savage ears
And plant in tyrants mild humility.

Love's Labor's Lost (4.3)

The Mystery of Love

"Tell me where is fancy bred,
Or in the heart or in the head?
How begot, how nourished?
      Reply, reply.
It is engend'red in the eyes.
With gazing fed, and fancy dies
In the cradle where it lies."

The Merchant of Venice (3.2)

          I know not why
I love this youth, and I have heard you say,
Love's reason's without reason.

Cymbeline (4.2)

Love's

Magic

She lov'd me for the dangers I had pass'd,
And I lov'd her that she did pity them.
This only is the witchcraft I have us'd.

The Tragedy of Othello, the Moor of Venice (1.3)

Speak low if you speak love.

Much Ado about Nothing (2.1)

The sight of lovers feedeth those in love.

As You Like It (3.4)

Things base and vile, holding no quantity,
Love can transpose to form and dignity.
Love looks not with the eyes but with the mind;
And therefore is wing'd Cupid painted blind.

A Midsummer Night's Dream (1.1)

5

Lovers and madmen have such seething brains,
Such shaping fantasies, that apprehend
More than cool reason ever comprehends.

A Midsummer Night's Dream (5.1)

I am giddy; expectation whirls me round;
Th' imaginary relish is so sweet
That it enchants my sense.

The History of Troilus and Cressida (3.2)

Courtship

Shall I command thy love?
I may. Shall I enforce thy love? I could. Shall I entreat
thy love? I will.

Love's Labor's Lost (4.1)

O mistress mine, where are you roaming?
O, stay and hear, your true-love's coming,
    That can sing both high and low.
Trip no further, pretty sweeting;
Journeys end in lovers meeting,
    Every wise man's son doth know.

Twelfth Night, or What You Will (2.3)

Viola.   If I did love you . . .
With such a suff'ring, such a deadly life,
In your denial I would find no sense,
I would not understand it.

Olivia.   Why, what would you?
Viola.   Make me a willow cabin at your
gate,
And call upon my soul within the house;
Write loyal cantons of contemned love,
And sing them loud even in the dead of night;
Hallow your name to the reverberate hills,
And make the babbling gossip of the air
Cry out "Olivia!" O, you should not rest
Between the elements of air and earth
But you should pity me!

Twelfth Night, or What You Will (1.5)

dear Kate, take a fellow of plain and un-
coin'd constancy, for he perforce must do thee right,
because he hath not the gift to woo in other places; for
these fellows of infinite tongue, that can rhyme them-
selves into ladies' favors, they do always reason them-
selves out again. What? a speaker is but a prater, a
rhyme is but a ballad; a good leg will fall, a straight
back will stoop, a black beard will turn white, a curl'd
pate will grow bald, a fair face will wither, a full eye
will wax hollow; but a good heart, Kate, is the sun
and the moon, or rather the sun and not the moon; for
it shines bright and never changes, but keeps his course
truly, If thou would have such a one, take me!

The Life of Henry the Fifth (5.2)

Plight me the full assurance of your faith,
That my most jealous and too doubtful soul
May live at peace.

Twelfth Night, or What You Will (4.3)

"A thousand kisses buys my heart from me,
And pay them at thy leisure, one by one.
What is ten hundred touches unto thee?
Are they not quickly told, and quickly gone?
    Say for non-payment that the debt should double,
    Is twenty hundred kisses such a trouble?"

Venus and Adonis (517–522)

First

Love

Did my heart love till now? Forswear it, sight!
For I ne'er saw true beauty till this night.

The Tragedy of Romeo and Juliet (1.5)

Even so quickly may one catch the plague?
Methinks I feel this youth's perfections
With an invisible and subtle stealth
To creep in at mine eyes. Well, let it be.

Twelfth Night, or What You Will (1.5)

Celia.   Come, come, wrastle with thy affections.
Rosalind.   Oh, they take the part of a better wrastler than myself!

As You Like It (1.3)

"Who ever lov'd that lov'd not at first sight?"

As You Like It (3.5)

Love's

Eagerness

lovers break not hours,
Unless it be to come before their time,
So much they spur their expedition.
See where she comes.

The Two Gentlemen of Verona (5.1)

it is marvel he out-dwells his hour,
For lovers ever run before the clock.

The Merchant of Venice (2.6)

The Pursuit
of Love

I pray, awake, sir; if you love the maid,
Bend thoughts and wits to achieve her.

The Taming of the Shrew (1.1)

in her bosom I'll unclasp my heart,
And take her hearing prisoner with the force
And strong encounter of my amorous tale.

Much Ado about Nothing (1.1)

Friendship is constant in all other things
Save in the office and affairs of love;
Therefore all hearts in love use their own tongues.
Let every eye negotiate for itself,
And trust no agent.

Much Ado about Nothing (2.1)

I have long lov'd her, and I protest to you, bestow'd much on her; follow'd her with a doting observance; engross'd opportunities to meet her; fee'd every slight occasion that could but niggardly give me sight of her; not only bought many presents to give her, but have given largely to many to know what she would have given; briefly, I have pursu'd her as love hath pursu'd me, which hath been on the wing of all occasions. But whatsoever I have merited, either in my mind or in my means, meed I am sure I have receiv'd none, unless experience be a jewel.

The Merry Wives of Windsor (2.2)

We cannot fight for love, as men may do.
We should be woo'd, and were not made to woo.

A Midsummer Night's Dream (2.1)

I'll be as patient as a gentle stream,
And make a pastime of each weary step,
Till the last step have brought me to my love,
And there I'll rest, as after much turmoil
A blessed soul doth in Elysium.

The Two Gentlemen of Verona (2.7)

*L*over's

*W*iles

Charmian.   Madam, methinks if you did love
him dearly,
You do not hold the method to enforce
The like from him.
    Cleopatra.   What should I do, I
do not?
    Charmian.   In each thing give him way, cross
him in nothing.
    Cleopatra.   Thou teachest like a fool: the way
to lose him.

The Tragedy of Antony and Cleopatra (1.3)

she belov'd knows nought that knows
    not this:
Men prize the thing ungain'd more than it is.

The History of Troilus and Cressida (1.2)

Cressida.　　　　　　I have lov'd you night
and day
For many weary months.
　　Troilus.　　Why was my Cressid then so hard
to win?
　　Cressida.　　Hard to seem won; but I was won,
my lord,
With the first glance that ever—pardon me,
If I confess much. . . .
　　　　　　　though I lov'd you well, I woo'd you
　not,
And yet, good faith, I wish'd myself a man,
Or that we women had men's privilege
Of speaking first.

The History of Troilus and Cressida (3.2)

If she do frown, 'tis not in hate of you,
But rather to beget more love in you.
If she do chide, 'tis not to have you gone,
For why, the fools are mad, if left alone.
Take no repulse, what ever she doth say;
For "get you gone," she doth not mean "away!"
. . .
That man that hath a tongue, I say is no man,
If with his tongue he cannot win a woman.

The Two Gentlemen of Verona (3.1)

Love's
Progress

your brother and my sister no sooner met
but they look'd; no sooner look'd but they lov'd; no
sooner lov'd but they sigh'd; no sooner sigh'd but they
ask'd one another the reason; no sooner knew the rea-
son but they sought the remedy: and in these degrees
have they made a pair of stairs to marriage, which they
will climb incontinent, or else be incontinent before
marriage. They are in the very wrath of love, and they
will together. Clubs cannot part them.

As You Like It (5.2)

We that are true lovers run into strange
capers.

As You Like It (2.4)

Obsessive

Love

If ever thou shalt love,
In the sweet pangs of it remember me;
For such as I am, all true lovers are,
Unstaid and skittish in all motions else,
Save in the constant image of the creature
That is belov'd.

Twelfth Night, or What You Will (2.4)

I am your spaniel . . .
The more you beat me, I will fawn on you.
Use me but as your spaniel; spurn me, strike me,
Neglect me, lose me; only give me leave,
Unworthy as I am, to follow you.

A Midsummer Night's Dream (2.1)

Love's

Folly

Love is your master, for he masters you;
And he that is so yoked by a fool,
Methinks should not be chronicled for wise.

The Two Gentlemen of Verona (1.1)

Love is merely a madness, and I tell you,
deserves as well a dark house and a whip as madmen
do; and the reason why they are not so punish'd and
cur'd is, that the lunacy is so ordinary that the whip-
pers are in love too.

As You Like It (3.2)

love is blind, and lovers cannot see
The pretty follies that themselves commit,
For if they could, Cupid himself would blush.

The Merchant of Venice (2.6)

If thou rememb'rest not the slightest folly
That ever love did make thee run into,
Thou hast not lov'd;
Or if thou hast not sat as I do now,
Wearing thy hearer in thy mistress' praise,
Thou hast not lov'd;
Or if thou hast not broke from company
Abruptly, as my passion now makes me,
Thou hast not lov'd.

As You Like It (2.4)

                    you are wise,
Or else you love not; for to be wise and love
Exceeds man's might; that dwells with gods above.

The History of Troilus and Cressida (3.2)

Valentine.   I have lov'd her ever since I saw
her, and still I see her beautiful.
Speed.   If you love her, you cannot see
her.
Valentine.   Why?
Speed.   Because Love is blind.

The Two Gentlemen of Verona (2.1)

I do much wonder that one man, seeing how much another man is a fool when he dedicates his behaviors to love, will, after he hath laugh'd at such shallow follies in others, become the argument of his own scorn by falling in love.

Much Ado about Nothing (2.3)

Love's Rocky
Course

Ay me! for aught that I could ever read,
Could ever hear by tale or history,
The course of true love never did run smooth.

A Midsummer Night's Dream (1.1)

Romeo.　　Is love a tender thing? It is too
　　rough,
Too rude, too boist'rous, and it pricks like thorn.
　Mercutio.　　If love be rough with you, be
　　rough with love.

The Tragedy of Romeo and Juliet (1.4)

Hope is a lover's staff; walk hence with that
And manage it against despairing thoughts.

The Two Gentlemen of Verona (3.1)

The

Kiss

"So sweet a kiss the golden sun gives not
To those fresh morning drops upon the rose,
As thy eye-beams, when their fresh rays have smote
The night of dew that on my cheeks down flows;
Nor shines the silver moon one half so bright
Through the transparent bosom of the deep."

Love's Labor's Lost (4.3)

Once he kiss'd me—
I lov'd my lips the better ten days after.
Would he would do so ev'ry day!

The Two Noble Kinsmen (2.4)

You have witchcraft in your lips, Kate;
there is more eloquence in a sugar touch of them than
in the tongues of the French council; and they should
sooner persuade Harry of England than a general pe-
tition of monarchs.

The Life of Henry the Fifth (5.5)

All Encompassing

Love

By him, like a shadow,
I'll ever dwell.

The Two Noble Kinsmen (2.6)

In love, i' faith, to the very tip of the nose.

The History of Troilus and Cressida (3.1)

Cleopatra.   If it be love indeed, tell me how
much.
Antony.   There's beggary in the love that
can be reckon'd.

The Tragedy of Antony and Cleopatra (1.1)

Sir, I love you more than [words] can
wield the matter,
Dearer than eyesight, space, and liberty,

Beyond what can be valued, rich or rare,
No less than life, with grace, health, beauty,
  honor;
As much as child e'er lov'd, or father found;
A love that makes breath poor, and speech
  unable:
Beyond all manner of so much I love you.

The Tragedy of King Lear (1.1)

Contrary

Love

I shall be lov'd when I am lack'd.

The Tragedy of Coriolanus (4.1)

Hermia.   I give him curses; yet he gives me love.
Helena.   O that my prayers could such affection move!
Hermia.   The more I hate, the more he follows me.
Helena.   The more I love, the more he hateth me.

A Midsummer Night's Dream (1.1)

What dangerous action, stood it next to death,
Would I not undergo for one calm look?

O, 'tis the curse in love, and still approv'd,
When women cannot love where they're
  belov'd!

The Two Gentlemen of Verona (5.4)

"Love like a shadow flies when substance love pursues,
pursuing that that flies, and flying what pursues."

The Merry Wives of Windsor (2.2)

Julia.   Why, he, of all the rest, hath never
    mov'd me.
Lucetta.   Yet he, of all the rest, I think best
    loves ye.
Julia.   His little speaking shows his love
    but small.
Lucetta.   Fire that's closest kept burns most
    of all.
Julia.   They do not love that do not show
    their love.
Lucetta.   O, they love least that let men
    know their love.
Julia.   I would I knew his mind.

The Two Gentlemen of Verona (1.2)

She dreams on him that has forgot her love;
You dote on her that cares not for your love.
'Tis pity love should be so contrary;
And thinking on it makes me cry "alas!"

The Two Gentlemen of Verona (4.4)

The Fullness
of Love

Two lovely berries moulded on one stem;
So with two seeming bodies, but one heart.

A Midsummer Night's Dream (3.2)

when that hour o'erslips me in the day
Wherein I sigh not, Julia, for thy sake,
The next ensuing hour some foul mischance
Torment me for my love's forgetfulness!

The Two Gentlemen of Verona (2.2)

as the sun is daily new and old,
So is my love still telling what is told.

Sonnets (76)

"Had I no eyes but ears, my ears would love
That inward beauty and invisible,
Or were I deaf, thy outward parts would move

Each part in me that were but sensible;
    Though neither eyes nor ears to hear nor see,
    Yet should I be in love by touching thee.

"Say that the sense of feeling were bereft me,
And that I could not see, nor hear, nor touch,
And nothing but the very smell were left me,
Yet would my love to thee be still as much."

Venus and Adonis (433–442)

In Praise of

the Beloved

she is mine own,
And I as rich in having such a jewel
As twenty seas, if all their sand were pearl,
The water nectar, and the rocks pure gold.

The Two Gentlemen of Verona (2.4)

His words are bonds, his oaths are oracles,
His love sincere, his thoughts immaculate,
His tears pure messengers sent from his heart,
His heart as far from fraud as heaven from earth.

The Two Gentlemen of Verona (2.7)

Age cannot wither her, nor custom stale
Her infinite variety. Other women cloy
The appetites they feed, but she makes hungry
Where most she satisfies.

The Tragedy of Antony and Cleopatra (2.2)

O, flatter me; for love delights in praises.

The Two Gentlemen of Verona (2.4)

Some glory in their birth, some in their skill,
Some in their wealth, some in their body's force,
Some in their garments, though new-fangled ill,
Some in their hawks and hounds, some in their horse;
And every humor hath his adjunct pleasure,
Wherein it finds a joy above the rest,
But these particulars are not my measure,
All these I better in one general best.
Thy love is [better] than high birth to me,
Richer than wealth, prouder than garments' cost,
Of more delight than hawks or horses be;
And having thee, of all men's pride I boast:
    Wretched in this alone, that thou mayst take
    All this away, and me most wretched make.

Sonnets (91)

One fairer than my love! The all-seeing sun
Ne'er saw her match since first the world begun.

The Tragedy of Romeo and Juliet (1.2)

If I could write the beauty of your eyes,
And in fresh numbers number all your graces,
The age to come would say, "This poet lies,
Such heavenly touches ne'er touch'd earthly faces."

Sonnets (17)

34

Love's
Delusions

Thus vainly thinking that she thinks me young,
Although she knows my days are past the best,
Simply I credit her false-speaking tongue;
On both sides thus is simple truth suppress'd.
But wherefore says she not she is unjust?
And wherefore say not I that I am old?
O, love's best habit is in seeming trust,
And age in love loves not t' have tears told.
　　Therefore I lie with her, and she with me,
　　And in our faults by lies we flattered be.

Sonnets (138)

O cunning Love, with tears thou keep'st me blind,
Lest eyes well seeing thy foul faults should find.

Sonnets (148)

Love's
Abandon

I [leave] myself, my friends, and all, for love.
Thou, Julia, thou hast metamorphis'd me,
Made me neglect my studies, lose my time,
War with good counsel, set the world at nought;
Made wit with musing weak, heart sick with thought.

The Two Gentlemen of Verona (1.1)

Jaques.   The worst fault you have is to be
     in love.
Orlando.   'Tis a fault I will not change for
     your best virtue.

As You Like It (3.2)

"Vows for thee broke deserve not punishment.
          what fool is not so wise
To lose an oath to win a paradise?"

Love's Labor's Lost (4.3)

were I crown'd the most imperial
monarch,
Thereof most worthy, were I the fairest youth
That ever made eye swerve, had force and knowledge
More than was ever man's, I would not prize them
Without her love.

The Winter's Tale (4.4)

Mockery of

Love

men have died from time to time, and
worms have eaten them, but not from love.

As You Like It (4.1)

Valentine.   Why, how know you that I am in
love?
Speed.   Marry, by these special marks:
first, you have learn'd . . . to wreathe your arms,
like a malecontent; to relish a love-song, like a robin-
redbreast; to walk alone, like one that had the
pestilence; to sigh, like a schoolboy that had lost his
A B C; to weep, like a young wench that had buried
her grandam; to fast, like one that takes diet; to
watch, like one that fears robbing.

The Two Gentlemen of Verona (2.1)

Princess.   We are wise girls to mock our
    lovers so.
Rosaline.   They are worse fools to purchase
    mocking so.

Love's Labor's Lost (5.2)

To marry him is hopeless;
To be his whore is witless. Out upon't!
What pushes are we wenches driven to
When fifteen once has found us!

The Two Noble Kinsmen (2.4)

Rosalind.   Now tell me how long you would
have her after you have possess'd her.
Orlando.   For ever and a day.
Rosalind.   Say "a day," without the "ever."
No, no, Orlando, men are April when they woo,
December when they wed; maids are May when
they are maids, but the sky changes when they are
wives.

As You Like It (4.1)

Some thousand verses of a faithful lover.
A huge translation of hypocrisy.

Love's Labor's Lost (5.2)

39

Passionate

Love

Olivia.   How does he love me?
Viola.   With adorations, fertile tears,
With groans that thunder love, with sighs of fire.

Twelfth Night, or What You Will (1.5)

This is the very ecstasy of love,
Whose violent property fordoes itself,
And leads the will to desperate undertakings
As oft as any passions under heaven
That does afflict our natures.

The Tragedy of Hamlet, Prince of Denmark (2.1)

They are but beggars that can count their worth,
But my true love is grown to such excess
I cannot sum up sum of half my wealth.

The Tragedy of Romeo and Juliet (2.6)

Perdition catch my soul
But I do love thee! and when I love thee not,
Chaos is come again.

The Tragedy of Othello, the Moor of Venice (3.3)

O love, be moderate, allay thy ecstasy,
In measure rain thy joy, scant this excess!
I feel too much thy blessing; make it less,
For fear I surfeit.

The Merchant of Venice (3.2)

　　　　her passions are made of nothing but the
finest part of pure love. We cannot call her winds and
waters sighs and tears; they are greater storms and
tempests than almanacs can report.

The Tragedy of Antony and Cleopatra (1.2)

Julia.　　　Thou wouldst as soon go kindle fire
　　with snow
As seek to quench the fire of love with words.
　　Lucetta.　　　I do not seek to quench your love's
　　hot fire,
But qualify the fire's extreme rage,
Lest it should burn above the bounds of reason.
　　Julia.　　　The more thou dam'st it up, the
　　more it burns.

The Two Gentlemen of Verona (2.7)

Affection is a coal that must be cool'd,
Else suffer'd it will set the heart on fire.
The sea hath bounds, but deep desire hath none.

Venus and Adonis (387–389)

Unrequited

Love

I know I love in vain, strive against hope;
Yet in this captious and intenible sieve
I still pour in the waters of my love
And lack not to lose still.

All's Well That Ends Well (1.3)

'Twere all one
That I should love a bright particular star
And think to wed it, he is so above me.
In his bright radiance and collateral light
Must I be comforted, not in his sphere.
Th' ambition in my love thus plagues itself:
The hind that would be mated by the lion
Must die for love.

All's Well That Ends Well (1.1)

she never told her love,
But let concealment, like a worm i' th' bud
Feed on her damask cheek; she pin'd in thought,

43

And with a green and yellow melancholy
She sate like Patience on a monument,
Smiling at grief. Was not this love indeed?

Twelfth Night, or What You Will (2.4)

O then give pity
To her whose state is such that cannot choose
But lend and give where she is sure to lose;
That seeks not to find that her search implies,
But riddle-like lives sweetly where she dies.

All's Well That Ends Well (1.3)

44

Love's

Torment

To be in love—where scorn is
bought with groans;
Coy looks with heart-sore sighs; one fading
moment's mirth
With twenty watchful, weary, tedious nights.

The Two Gentlemen of Verona (1.1)

What, do I love her,
That I desire to hear her speak again?
And feast upon her eyes? . . .
Never could the strumpet,
With all her double vigor, art and nature,
Once stir my temper; but this virtuous maid
Subdues me quite. Ever till now,
When men were fond, I smil'd and wond'red how.

Measure for Measure (2.2)

If ever (as that ever may be near)
You meet in some fresh cheek the power of
     fancy,
Then shall you know the wounds invisible
That love's keen arrows make.

As You Like It (3.5)

Benvolio.   What sadness lengthens Romeo's
     hours?
Romeo.   Not having that which, having,
     makes them short.
Benvolio.   In love?
Romeo.   Out—
Benvolio.   Of love?
Romeo.   Out of her favor where I am in
     love.
Benvolio.   Alas that love, so gentle in his
     view,
Should be so tyrannous and rough in proof!

The Tragedy of Romeo and Juliet (1.1)

Rosalind.   There is none of my uncle's marks
upon you. He taught me how to know a man in
love; in which cage of rushes I am sure you [are]
not prisoner.
     Orlando.   What were his marks?
     Rosalind.   A lean cheek, which you have
not; a blue eye and sunken, which you have not; an

47

unquestionable spirit, which you have not; a beard
neglected, which you have not . . . then your hose
should be ungarter'd, your bonnet unbanded, your
sleeve unbutton'd, your shoe untied, and every
thing about you demonstrating a careless
desolation.

As You Like It (3.2)

I have done penance for contemning Love,
Whose high imperious thoughts have punish'd me
With bitter fasts, with penitential groans,
With nightly tears, and daily heart-sore sighs,
For in revenge of my contempt of love,
Love hath chas'd sleep from my enthralled eyes,
And made them watchers of mine own heart's sorrow.
O . . . Love's a mighty lord.

The Two Gentlemen of Verona (2.4)

'Tis pity love should be so tyrannous.

The Two Noble Kinsmen (4.2)

Mercutio.　　You are a lover, borrow Cupid's
　　wings,
And soar with them above a common bound.
　　Romeo.　　I am too sore enpierced with his
　　shaft

48

To soar with his light feathers, and so bound
I cannot bound a pitch above dull woe;
Under love's heavy burthen do I sink.

The Tragedy of Romeo and Juliet (1.4)

Love's

Secrecy

"Art thou asham'd to kiss? then wink again,
And I will wink, so shall the day seem night.
Love keeps his revels where there are but twain;
Be bold to play, our sport is not in sight;
    These blue-vein'd violets whereon we lean
    Never can blab, nor know not what we mean."

Venus and Adonis (121–126)

Loquacious

Love

Thou wilt be like a lover presently,
And tire the hearer with a book of words.

Much Ado about Nothing (1.1)

Her song was tedious, and outwore the night,
For lovers' hours are long, though seeming short;
If pleas'd themselves, others may think delight
In such-like circumstance, with such-like sport.
Their copious stories, oftentimes begun,
End without audience, and are never done.

Venus and Adonis (841–846)

A murd'rous guilt shows not itself more soon
Than love that would seem hid: love's night is noon.

Twelfth Night, or What You Will (3.1)

Parting

Good night, good night! Parting is such sweet sorrow,
That I shall say good night till it be morrow.

The Tragedy of Romeo and Juliet (2.2)

Since I have your good leave to go away,
I will make haste; but till I come again,
No bed shall e'er be guilty of my stay,
Nor rest be interposer 'twixt us twain.

The Merchant of Venice (3.2)

How like a winter hath my absence been
From thee, the pleasure of the fleeting year!
What freezings have I felt, what dark days seen!
What old December's bareness every where! . . .
For summer and his pleasures wait on thee,
And thou away, the very birds are mute;
    Or if they sing, 'tis with so dull a cheer
    That leaves look pale, dreading the winter's near.

Sonnets (97)

Juliet.   'Tis almost morning, I would have
          thee gone—
And yet no farther than a wanton's bird,
That lets it hop a little from his hand,
Like a poor prisoner in his twisted gyves,
And with a silken thread plucks it back again,
So loving-jealous of his liberty.
     Romeo.   I would I were thy bird.
     Juliet.   Sweet, so would I,
Yet I should kill thee with much cherishing.

The Tragedy of Romeo and Juliet (2.2)

Love goes toward love as schoolboys from their books,
But love from love, toward school with heavy looks.

The Tragedy of Romeo and Juliet (2.2)

Vows of

Love

Lady, as you are mine, I am yours. I give
away myself for you, and dote upon the exchange.

Much Ado about Nothing (2.1)

Thee will I love and with thee lead my life;
Thou hast no husband yet, nor I no wife.

The Comedy of Errors (3.2)

O gentle Romeo,
If thou dost love, pronounce it faithfully;
Or if thou thinkest I am too quickly won,
I'll frown and be perverse . . .
But trust me, gentleman, I'll prove more true
Than those that have [more] coying to be strange.
        . . . therefore pardon me,
And not impute this yielding to light love,
Which the dark night hath so discovered.

The Tragedy of Romeo and Juliet (2.2)

Lysander.   One turf shall serve as pillow for
        us both,
One heart, one bed, two bosoms, and one troth.
    Hermia.   Nay, [good] Lysander; for my
        sake, my dear,
Lie further off yet; do not lie so near.
    Lysander.   O, take the sense, sweet, of my
        innocence!
        . . . I mean, that my heart unto yours
        [is] knit,
So that but one heart we can make of it;
Two bosoms interchained with an oath,
So then two bosoms and a single troth. . . .
    Hermia.   . . . So far be distant; and good
        night, sweet friend.
Thy love ne'er alter till thy sweet life end!

A Midsummer Night's Dream (2.2)

Who then recovers. Say thou art mine, and ever
My love, as it begins, shall so persever.

All's Well That Ends Well (4.2)

Love

Disdained

"Remove your siege from my unyielding heart,
To love's alarms it will not ope the gate;
   Dismiss your vows, your feigned tears, your flatt'ry,
   For where a heart is hard they make no
      batt'ry."

Venus and Adonis (423–426)

   I had rather hear my dog bark at a crow
than a man swear he loves me.

Much Ado about Nothing (1.1)

   Sweet Phebe, do not scorn me, do not,
Phebe;
Say that you love me not, but say not so
In bitterness. The common executioner,
Whose heart th' accustom'd sight of death makes
   hard,

Falls not the axe upon the humbled neck
But first begs pardon. Will you sterner be
Than he that dies and lives by bloody drops?

As You Like It (3.5)

    I pray you do not fall in love with me,
For I am falser than vows made in wine.

As You Like It (3.5)

Forbidden

Love

Falstaff.   Have you receiv'd no promise of
satisfaction at her hands?
Ford.   Never.
Falstaff.   Have you importun'd her to such a
purpose?
Ford.   Never.
Falstaff.   Of what quality was your love
then?
Ford.   Like a fair house built on another
man's ground, so that I have lost my edifice by
mistaking the place where I erected it.

The Merry Wives of Windsor (2.2)

Love's
Frailty

O, how this spring of love resembleth
The uncertain glory of an April day,
Which now shows all the beauty of the sun,
And by and by a cloud takes all away.

The Two Gentlemen of Verona (1.3)

love moderately: long love doth so;
Too swift arrives as tardy as too slow.

The Tragedy of Romeo and Juliet (2.6)

"The tender spring upon thy tempting lip
Shows thee unripe; yet mayst thou well be tasted.
Make use of time, let not advantage slip,
Beauty within itself should not be wasted.
   Fair flowers that are not gath'red in their prime
   Rot, and consume themselves in little time."

Venus and Adonis (127–132)

O happiness enjoy'd but of a few,
And if possess'd, as soon decay'd and done
As is the morning's silver melting dew
Against the golden splendor of the sun!
An expir'd date, cancell'd ere well begun.
    Honor and beauty, in the owner's arms,
    Are weakly fortress'd from a world of harms.

The Rape of Lucrece (22–28)

Jealousy

O, beware, my lord, of jealousy!
It is the green-ey'd monster, which doth mock
The meat it feeds on. That cuckold lives in bliss
Who, certain of his fate, loves not his wronger;
But O, what damned minutes tells he o'er
Who dotes, yet doubts; suspects, yet [strongly] loves!

The Tragedy of Othello, the Moor of Venice (3.3)

How many fond fools serve mad jealousy?

The Comedy of Errors (2.1)

Desdemona.   Alas the day, I never gave him
        cause.
Emilia.   But jealous souls will not be
        answer'd so;
They are not ever jealous for the cause,
But jealous for they're jealous. It is a monster
Begot upon itself, born on itself.

The Tragedy of Othello, the Moor of Venice (3.4)

63

"This sour informer, this bate-breeding spy,
This canker that eats up Love's tender spring,
This carry-tale, dissentious Jealousy,
That sometime true news, sometime false doth bring,
    Knocks at my heart."

Venus and Adonis (655–659)

"where Love reigns, disturbing Jealousy
Doth call himself Affection's sentinel,
Gives false alarms, suggesteth mutiny,
And in a peaceful hour doth cry, 'Kill, Kill!'
    Distemp'ring gentle Love in his desire,
    As air and water do abate the fire."

Venus and Adonis (649–654)

Trifles light as air
Are to the jealous confirmations strong
As proofs of holy writ.

The Tragedy of Othello, the Moor of Venice (3.3)

The Power of
Love

they say base men being in love have then
a nobility in their natures more than is native to them.

The Tragedy of Othello, the Moor of Venice (2.1)

love makes young men thrall, and old
men dote.

Venus and Adonis (837)

The Curse
of Love

"Sorrow on love hereafter shall attend;
It shall be waited on with jealousy,
Find sweet beginning, but unsavory end;
    Ne'er settled equally, but high or low,
    That all love's pleasure shall not match his
woe."

Venus and Adonis (1136–1140)

"It shall be fickle, false, and full of fraud,
Bud, and be blasted, in a breathing while,
The bottom poison, and the top o'erstraw'd
With sweets that shall the truest sight beguile;
    The strongest body shall it make most weak,
    Strike the wise dumb, and teach the fool to
        speak.

"It shall be sparing, and too full of riot,
Teaching decrepit age to tread the measures;
The staring ruffian shall it keep in quiet,

Pluck down the rich, enrich the poor with treasures;
    It shall be raging mad, and silly mild,
    Make the young old, the old become a child.

"It shall suspect where is no cause of fear,
It shall not fear where it should most mistrust,
It shall be merciful, and too severe,
And most deceiving when it seems most just;
    Perverse it shall be, where it shows most
        toward,
    Put fear to valor, courage to the coward.

"It shall be cause of war and dire events,
And set dissension 'twixt the son and sire,
Subject and servile to all discontents,
As dry combustious matter is to fire.
    Sith in his prime, Death doth my love destroy,
    They that love best, their loves shall not enjoy."

Venus and Adonis (1141–1164)

Love's

Understanding

No more be griev'd at that which thou hast done:
Roses have thorns, and silver fountains mud,
Clouds and eclipses stain both moon and sun,
And loathsome canker lives in sweetest bud.
All men make faults, and even I in this.

Sonnets (35)

Love

Lost

love that comes too late,
Like a remorseful pardon slowly carried,
To the great sender turns a sour offense,
Crying, "That's good that's gone."

All's Well That Ends Well (5.3)

Lord. . . . Thou hast a
lady far more beautiful
Than any woman in this waning age.
1. Servant. And till the tears that she hath
shed for thee
Like envious floods o'errun her lovely face,
She was the fairest creature in the world,

The Taming of the Shrew (Induction. 2)

"Alas, poor world, what treasure hast thou lost!
What face remains alive that's worth the viewing?
Whose tongue is music now? what canst thou boast

Of things long since, or any thing ensuing?
   The flowers are sweet, their colors fresh and trim,
   But true sweet beauty liv'd and died with him."

Venus and Adonis (1075–1080)

Ruin hath taught me thus to ruminate,
That Time will come and take my love away.
   This thought is as a death, which cannot choose
   But weep to have that which it fears to lose.

Sonnets (64)

         now he's gone, and my idolatrous fancy
Must sanctify his reliques.

All's Well That Ends Well (1.1)

*B*etrayal

She's gone. I am abus'd, and my relief
Must be to loathe her. O curse of marriage!
That we can call these delicate creatures ours,
And not their appetites!

The Tragedy of Othello, the Moor of Venice (3.3)

What sense had I in her stol'n hours of lust?
I saw't not, thought it not; it harm'd not me.
I slept the next night well, fed well, was free and merry;
I found not Cassio's kisses on her lips. . . .
. . . I had been happy, if the general camp,
Pioners and all, had tasted her sweet body,
So I had nothing known. O now, for ever
Farewell the tranquil mind!

The Tragedy of Othello, the Moor of Venice (3.3)

'Tis so strange,
That, though the truth of it stands off as gross
As black and white, my eye will scarcely see it.

The Life of Henry the Fifth (2.2)

Sweetest things turn sourest by
their deeds;
Lilies that fester smell far worse than weeds.

Sonnets (94)

My blood is mingled with the crime of lust;
For if we two be one, and thou play false,
I do digest the poison of thy flesh,
Being strumpeted by thy contagion.
Keep then fair league and truce with thy true bed.

The Comedy of Errors (2.2)

Chastity

'Tis a commodity will lose the gloss with lying: the longer kept, the less worth . . . your virginity, your old virginity, is like one of our French wither'd pears, it looks ill, it eats drily, marry, 'tis a wither'd pear; it was formerly better, marry, yet 'tis a wither'd pear. Will you any thing with it?

All's Well That Ends Well (1.1)

I must tell you friendly in your ear,
Sell when you can, you are not for all markets.
Cry the man mercy, love him, take his offer.

As You Like It (3.5)

she'll not be hit
With Cupid's arrow, she hath Dian's wit;
And in strong proof of chastity well arm'd,
From Love's weak childish bow she lives uncharm'd.
She will not stay the siege of loving terms,

Nor bide th' encounter of assailing eyes,
Nor ope her lap to saint-seducing gold.
O, she is rich in beauty, only poor
That, when she dies, with beauty dies her store.

The Tragedy of Romeo and Juliet (1.1)

What's this? what's this? Is this her fault, or mine?
The tempter, or the tempted, who sins most?

Measure for Measure (2.2)

Lust

"Love comforteth like sunshine after rain,
But Lust's effort is tempest after sun;
Love's gentle spring doth always fresh remain,
Lust's winter comes ere summer half be done;
Love surfeits not, Lust like a glutton dies;
Love is all truth, Lust full of forged lies."

Venus and Adonis (799–804)

[Lust], though to a radiant angel link'd,
Will [sate] itself in a celestial bed
And prey on garbage.

The Tragedy of Hamlet, Prince of Denmark (1.5)

Fie on sinful fantasy!
Fie on lust and luxury!
Lust is but a bloody fire,
Kindled with unchaste desire,
Fed in heart, whose flames aspire,

As thoughts do blow them, higher and
     higher.
Pinch him, fairies, mutually!
Pinch him for his villainy!
Pinch him, and burn him, and turn him about,
Till candles, and starlight, and moonshine be
     out.

The Merry Wives of Windsor (5.5)

'Tis one thing to be tempted . . .
Another thing to fall.

Measure for Measure (2.1)

Self

Love

Self-love, my liege, is not so vile a sin
As self-neglecting.

The Life of Henry the Fifth (2.4)

She cannot love,
Nor take no shape nor project of affection,
She is so self-endeared.

Much Ado about Nothing (3.1)

Sin of self-love possesseth all mine eye,
And all my soul, and all my every part;
And for this sin there is no remedy,
It is so grounded inward in my heart.

Sonnets (62)

O, you are sick of self-love . . . and taste with a distemper'd appetite.

Twelfth Night, or What You Will (1.5)

Love loving not itself, none other can.

The Tragedy of King Richard the Second (5.3)

Unending

Love

My bounty is as boundless as the sea,
My love as deep; the more I give to thee,
The more I have, for both are infinite.

The Tragedy of Romeo and Juliet (2.2)

Unkindness may do much,
And his unkindness may defeat my life,
But never taint my love.

The Tragedy of Othello, the Moor of Venice (4.2)

Let me not to the marriage of true minds
Admit impediments; love is not love
Which alters when it alteration finds,
Or bends with the remover to remove.
O no, it is an ever-fixed mark
That looks on tempests and is never shaken;
It is the star to every wand'ring bark,

Whose worth's unknown, although his highth be
   taken.
Love's not Time's fool, though rosy lips and cheeks
Within his bending sickle's compass come,
Love alters not with his brief hours and weeks,
But bears it out even to the edge of doom.
     If this be error and upon me proved,
     I never writ, nor no man ever loved.

Sonnets (116)

O, never say that I was false of heart,
Though absence seem'd my flame to qualify;
As easy might I from myself depart
As from my soul which in thy breast doth lie.

Sonnets (109)

To me, fair friend, you never can be old,
For as you were when first your eye I ey'd,
Such seems your beauty still.

Sonnets (104)

Give me your hands.
Receive you her, you him, be plighted with
A love that grows as you decay.

The Two Noble Kinsmen (5.3)

About Shakespeare

William Shakespeare was born in Stratford, England, in 1564 and died, presumably there, on his fifty-second birthday, on April 23, 1616. When in his mid-twenties, he went to London, where he wrote his plays, his sonnets, and other poems.

It is known that Shakespeare's plays were successful in their day, that he acted in some of them, and that he came to the attention of royalty. However, puzzlingly little else has been found out about him, less than about a great many of his contemporaries.

But though we know little about Shakespeare, he knew a stunning amount about us, and we attend his plays or read him both for pleasure and to learn about ourselves.